Green Path: 2018 Revolution, 2020 Vision

By Al R Suarez

Table of Contents

Intro

As is tradition I would like to dedicate this book to a person, sometimes I do multiple persons or to someone who has passed away. This person is an indivual very much alive in my life, Steven Machat. I have not talked about this publicly, but he facilitated my trip to Standing Rock, which brought about a transformation in my life. His friend in Minneapolis took me in and gave me the supplies I needed for the trip in the dead of winter. For this, and much more, as I meet with Machat in our ongoing events in Miami, gives me immense gratitude, so this book published in Miami, where our Atlantis Revolution will emergy, where we will save the ocean, Godwilling, is dedicated to him. His passion for music, law and politics is blended in a revolutionary alliance we will form together.

The plans for this book started in December 2016 in Tampa, little did I know then within three months I would be uprooted, and come to Miami, to continue my activism. The process of studying, and dealing with the uprooting, postponed much of my plans, including for publishing the book. I will go further in the book into the details to how this happened in the Infiltration chapter as it is related to Green matters. The audience for this book I want primarily to be Green Party members, especially in the US. First on a positive note, I want to get into the optimism I still feel inspite of everything, determined as ever, into the new path the Greens are taking, which is quite revolutionary, and has many historical paralells, and convinces me this strategy will work in the long-run.

Yes the long-run, the vision, that revolutionaries have, that whether they win or lose, will continue with steadfast devotion to the cause of causes, environmental protection, prevention of catastrophe, but also social justice, equality and the like. Among the descriptions of the word steadfast in the dictionary, is firmness. Firmness in particular is essential to the survival of our oganization, which has existed since the Orwellian year of my birth 1984, 84' being the year of the formation of the Green Party USA, not to be confused with GP USA, which is a group that later separated from the Green Party itself, where they pay dues, etc.

Part of the new course of the Greens has been inspired by dear friend and comrade, Cheri Honkala, who while I write this is fighting tooth and nail for a seat as a State Rep in Philadelphia in an emergency election. The two prior people in that position, Democrats, have both been tried for corruption, the latter candidate was actually convicted a year ago but did not have to reveal it or do her sentence till a year later, where she is now forced to step down, much like Debbie Wasserman-Shultz as DNC chair for electoral corruption, only she somehow got reelected here in Florida for Congress, but we will go into that.

There is a similar election going on in California right now with a Green candidate I need to learn more about. Even before the 2018 local elections, Greens are fighting to have their voices heard already. This new voice is that of the poor and working class, including people of color from the ghettos and barrios of the inner city, who want an alternative party to champion their cause of social justice, I should say, our cause, as I feel part of this group.

Miami, Florida

March 7th 2017

Chapter I Building The Coalition, Achieving Power

I often refer to a permanent opposition (until we get someone in power) but I want to put emphasis on coalition. Since coalitions or united fronts would not strictly have Greens, but have people with the same principles as us, want the same society, but may differ on tactics, which is something to be negotiated, principles however cannot be negotiated. Greens are often invited to Democrat events and are pushed to the side, not allowed to speak, and are passive about it. We need self-confidence, to have our own events, our own security as I have seen we have when Jill Stein comes to town. For once, Democrats who are progressive should come to our events, not the other way around. To achieve power, and the aim of power, it must be discussed.

One must not give into power but must tip toe, always taking consultation from others. Once power is reached it must be given to the people, true democracy. As the word democracy, from the Greeks, means power to the people. Sometimes the last step is forgotten, and as they say, absolute power is achieved, which corrupts absolutely in its excess. Some had good intentions but have gone mad from power. Others who were Machiavellian and scheming the whole time letting themselves be underestimated, learning, being opportunistic, take advantage. Some Anarchists believe power should not be the aim at all, that the opposition must be permanent. Am more of a Marx than a Chomsky, I disagree with this notion. Ultimately I want Greens to win, get power, I believe they are the best. But to get there we need to work with other people with similar aims, and put ego to the side. As I write this book, am getting positions already with Miami Greens for the benefit of our power, and society, best of both worlds, both at my college, and at the Green local, while in Tampa infiltrators plotted against me, here am making progress.

No longer in Tampa, am situated where I feel I can effect change more, where you are matters in forming a revolution, where it calls, you go, from your soul, like when I went to Standing Rock to fight the pipeline, as we have our own pipelines here, as I write these words we plan actions and marches from Naples to Miami to fight the Sabal pipeline, including with others who were in Standing Rock, ND, as Native or Native allies against the evil corporations who would threaten the water sipply of 18 million Americans. So let us find ways to recruit people to our cause. It's not about personalities, but we must be outgoing and passionate, not obsessive or aggressive, in getting the masses, patiently explaining to them as Lenin put it, how a Green economy is relevant to them and can change everything for the greater good as Stein puts it.

Chapter II Infiltration

Originally this chapter had a photo from the Matrix but there was not enough room. Also below where there is photos one taken of Stein and me in 2013 could not fit, it can be seen on my facebook. We often see infiltrators, also known as agent provocateurs, that familiar phrase coming from the French, as traitorus, as trator is part of the name making that word come to mind, but also as subhuman, like the agents in the Matrix chasing Neo. I have discussed them at length in my other books, and they are an ongoing problem, often ignored, as to not seem like a paranoid conspiracy theorist, but it is an issue that must be confronted head on. In Standing Rock someone described the armed police and mercenaries who brutalized peaceful water protectors, as people with no emotion, subhuman in a way. Many of the protectors did not see them that way. We need leadership, discipline, and to organize to prevent further infiltration, and yes kick the infiltrators exposed out, but with evidence, as we do not want to make the mistakes of the past and kick innocents out, letting ourselves going beyond the realm of paranoia to vigilance.

I am now going to share my blog where I expose the infiltration in Tampa causing me to make a tactical retreat, what it does not mention is that later Francisco, president of Green Party Alliance club at my college orchestrated a coup against me, wrote lies to the Dean, had me banned from all clubs and student extra curriculer activities. But these opposing forces only had me go to Miami, where our Atlantis type revolution, a spiritual one at that, will come about, with true allies like Steven Machat (ran for Senate in 2016 as an independent, a Green ally and ally of mine) and others, we will lead the way to liberty. Below will also be my blog on the infamous Donna Davis. By the way the guy who was in charge of outrage Jason, left the local, he made a mistake over Donna, but is an ally, am doing outreach down here as well. He and others have left the Tampa Green local since then, and want me to help them start a new one, but it is too late, am down here, I wish them well. Between the two blogs are some photos which will be like an intermission, since they are intense, but truthful, a truth many do not want to accept, but it is my truth.

https://alrsuarez.wordpress.com/2016/12/30/how-ahmad-saadaldin-used-a-space-party-apparatus-to-divide-a-movement/

Photo of Ahmad as appears on his LinkedIn (title in link, photo above)

It is hard to believe one person can do so much damage. What opportunists, and those who want to get money and fame from the Green movement, will do to destroy others. It would be unfair to say it was all Ahmad. He has accomplices. Some of them will be exposed in this article, others will be in my upcoming book Green Path as mentioned on this blog. I am for the path of unity, but those who constantly seek division over dialogue must be exposed, those who will work with infiltrators, and not see the error of their ways, I have lost tolerance for. I hope my other blog posts can be less controversial, but I find this necessary.

On the night of the election, November 8th, after working at the voter booth all day, I went to the Peace House, a space Ahmad rents here in Tampa, where the Green local and Green Party events are held, to meet with my Green comrades. The next night I gave a speech, which was posted in this blog. In the speech I mention briefly the infiltration of Donna Davis, as in this blog, and subsequently a few days later I confronted Donna on video when she attempted to lead a "anti Trump" protest in my neighborhood in Ybor, where many of the protesters were paid to go to which is against my principles. Exposing Donna I knew would cost me, she is backed by powerful people, but the extent of the cost I had no idea would be this bad. The video was later erased. I did it for unity, not that I was afraid BLM would file suite against me, which I was threatened with.   I am a supporter of BLM, Donna is a person not a movement. I have little means, and what I said was factual, so I have nothing to fear, nor does this article give anyone the right to suite since it is reality as I see it.

In the vid I simply ask Donna as she is walking off the stage as many of you had seen: "How does it feel to have sold out to Hillary and for her to still have lost?" She then sent a security guy who tried to kick me out rather than answer a question I asked

Photo of Donna and Jill was too big, not worth showing anyway, is seen on blog.

NOVEMBER 5, 2016   EDIT

Co Founder of BLM Tampa Betrays Community And Becomes Head Canvasser For   Hillary

Cynical Donna Davis, who worked for Hillary the whole time, poses with Jill Stein in Tampa (I was there interacting with Stein and Donna at the same time), days before she turned the corporation she directs "Sunshine State Voters" from a non partisan voter registration group to a door to door for Hillary!

I texted Donna letting her know I found out and would write about it, wanted to get a quote from her to no avail. Donna was a keynote speaker at the Stein event in Tampa! What a joke. I talked to the man who invited her, and we are all regretful this happened, and will take proper steps to better organize our events. Precautions, prevention of infiltration, is essential, as we continue post election for our movement to progress. What irony, as I gave Donna one of the books I wrote which has a focus on infiltration!

Having protested with Donna this year and working with her for about a month and a half at Sunshine State Voters, I always assumed she was a real activist. Someone I admired. I understand people need to earn money, to support their families. But if I was on the street (I been homeless) I would still refuse a dime from Hillary. What Donna has done is worse than a prostitute, who sells their body, she sold her soul. This is the real reason

When I asked presidential candidate for the Green Party Jill Stein a question in Miami September 2016, after seeing her in Tampa.

Jill Stein and me in Tampa 2016

was used to get me out. It was never a secret am an activist. This is the damage to my political life Ahmad has helped set up.

Francisco however, when we worked together, confided in me with some things as well, like Richard called Kim O'Connor a drunk. Apparently, he does not respect 125,000 people in our county voted for her and spreads rumors like Ahmad! Well, Kim confided in me after the vid came out that at the Cuban Club to try to shut up Kim from cheering for Stein, Donna threatened to break her legs! Kim also confirmed to me Richard asked her about this after I told him during mediation, and she said it was true, and yet he still does not want me at the Green local for offending a non Green Donna, who threatened our elected official twice her age! If this is not infiltration I do not know what is. When you read my post on Donna, you will be shocked, and more so how it has been handled ever since. This is the first time on my blog am coming out about the threat. Francisco, who is now buddys with Ahmad, said to me I should read the whole speech, Ahmad is not on the council, but me being reasonable I cut it anyway, for what? For Ahmad to cause this damage? And now Kim has been intimidated, she did not show up to get me to bring me to a St Pete Greens meeting, my last card is now dealt. This article and legal action are my only options. A guy known as Jason K asked Richard about the appeal, at the local, and Richard said I would have to ask him directly. Its clear Richard is avoiding an answer. Other Greens, especially those who have gone to Standing Rock for our revolution, have experienced similar things, being discredited, let us learn from this, deal with the infiltrators and their accomplices, and unite for the cause! If tribes in Standing Rock who have killed each other's families for centuries can unite, so can we! I hope my next post is a positive one. May the New Year be one of unity!

*Since this article was originally posted Ms. O'Connor got back in touch with me, she could not pick me up over a miscommunication, she is still very much an ally. I decided to keep the article since the Greens could have had their meetings at the library again, but instead sided with the provocateur Ahmad, who is a tool of the upper class elites on the council who run things when this is supposed to be a party of the people.

However, Ahmad said something in the correspondence that set me off. He said it could bore members, to hear about activism. Me having been on the frontlines of various activist causes at home or abroad for 15 years I took offense. I asked if he meant my activism was boring. He ignored me. I added Francisco to the convo so he could see himself what he said. I told Ahmad he may have not been a activist, he could just be a Green partisan, but I was concerned he was saying members activism could bore others. Finally Ahmad responded saying I would watch the meeting from the window if I continued to be disrespectful. I explained it was not my intent to be disrespectful, that I would see him that night that I cut the speech in half as he asked. To my amazement he suddenly said "Don't come, I don't want to see you tonight." I offered him my number in case he wanted to talk to clear things up, the call never came.

I then made the mistake of reaching out to Richard Carpenter. I had been warned about him before, about his racist remarks made Connie Burton not speak at the Cuban Club when Stein came to town, about how he had venue changed last moment resulting in dozens of people not being able to attend. Me being a person who does not like to pre-judge, I gave Richard the benefit of the doubt. Even ended up liking him. I later realized I should have listened to their advice. Richard pretended to be sympathetic, when all along he was using my words against me, and making sure Ahmad's side, not mine, would be heard, as he admitted that the council only heard his side, and promised to see about an appeal, which to this day weeks later he has not got back to me on. I later found out the "bylaws" Richard said he would look at or send me, do not exist yet. Kim O'Connor, an elected Green official in our area herself confirmed his fraud. I told Richard that Ahmad volunteered info to me, about pot, that he was acting stupid. At no point however, did I say I would ever speak to his landlord, and I still have not. If words gets to him this was of Ahmad's creation not mine.   It is legal now anyway medicinally in Florida.

Anyway the "mediation" Richard was doing after a couple weeks was not going well, I still was not going to Green local meets, and I focused on efforts at the Green club at my college. Finally I wrote Ahmad directly. I told   him that I am a patient man, I reminded him what he said to me about pot, but said am not the type of person who would go to his landlord. He then took this as a threat (if he believes his own lies) and said I was a filthy drunk, and he would call the cops (apparently who he is a snitch for) if I showed up at the Peace House. That I was yelling at our "allies" on the street (this could only be in reference to the vid, but there was no yelling). I informed Richard of this, and he said he would have to talk to the council.

A few days later I get a text from Richard saying because of what I did to Donna, and for "harassing" Ahmad my active member form would not be accepted. From there I discovered Francisco was using my words against me to Ahmad, and Francisco sent me a text a few days later saying I could not attend meetings at my own club at my college! I was first told it was because he did not like my posts online, even though mention of these problems have been minimal, and he did it in a way against the club constitution I helped set up. Later, I found out a former member did not like my "activism", and that autonomously as a reporter, which is my right. The guy who tried to kick me out whose name escapes me his name I exposed in a comment on the article exposing Donna. Am not going to get into her infiltration, people are free to see the post, but she is connected to Ahmad which is why I mention it.

Anyway, in the process of going to the Peace House, I admit in the parking lot outside the building after working all day,   I had a beer in my friend's car, Ahmad asked I not bring it in since the owner is a strict Muslim, and I said fine.   He then proceeded to tell me that he smokes pot in the place,   and the owner does not know. He later used this to call me a "filthy drunk". Why he volunteered this information to me on his pot smoking I don't know. He may believe in Sharia law, but to try to impose it in any way, or use the fact I drank a beer to stain my character is unacceptable.

After the video where I question Donna, I knew Jason Bardoux (his last name he uses I found out is fake) would want to talk to me. He is the man who made the mistake of inviting Donna to the Cuban Club, and was recently made by the council in charge of outreach (the council are a bunch of old white guys run by the infamous Richard Carpenter who do not believe in consensus, and make decisions without consulting active members or having existent bylaws, their existence is based on fraud). Richard helped mediate between Jason and myself, and Jason understood as I acting on principle, and my action, which I did with Francisco mind you, president of the Green club at my college of which I was VP, was autonomous, therefore I did not need to consult with him or the council.

While this mediation was going on outside, Ahmad was off in the distance listening. Before that I wrote him asking what he thought of the vid, all correspondence with him I can show with screenshot upon request, and he said I should keep the enemy closer, I took that as a way of saying back off, which was my intent, I was not going to write more about Donna, of course circumstances she is partially responsible have forced my hand. Ahmad has abused his authority, Donna had made a threat against a current Green elected official I found out later, which I will expose here. Little did I know Ahmad, was actually resentful of my autonomous action, and did not like my speech of November 9th, saying we needed to work on our mentality of Democratic reform,   towards Green revolutionary thinking. At the local that night we had more members than ever present, about 30, it is sad how Ahmad has divided things up for his benefit, already people have left because of how I was treated, and there is talk of starting a new local. Since my return from Standing Rock more than a month since   my differences with Ahmad, all my attempts at further mediation have come to nothing.

Anyway, after the brutal attacks in Standing Rock of November 20th, I thought Ahmad who told me in the past Standing Rock was not a priority, would finally led up and let me give a speech on Standing Rock (he is not a member of the council, but acts like one, out of respect I sent him my speech in advance and consulted with him). He said to take out all references of my activism, that would effectively cut the speech in half and make it a 2 minute announcement, me being reasonable, I agreed.

why I was not rehired for this mysterious new name of the corporation to go "door to door" she knew I would say no, they are canvassing for Hillary! This is someone I consider worse than Trump. The follow up article will show the evidence of the funds Donna is getting. What makes me sick is that the "non partisan" group I worked for, could have had me indirectly funded from the Hillary campaign against my will. When I ended working this summer at Community Voters Project, I was offered to canvass for Hillary, they told me, we don't like Hillary either, but they tell you what to say, they pay you, I said no.

This was against my principles. It is no wonder Donna laughed when I asked her why I would not be rehired even though I had top numbers for people who registered to vote. She said I caused "drama". She knew I would say no. The fact she arrogantly thinks she can get away with this, and ever pass for an activist again, is astounding. Donna needs to be shunned from our Green events, activist events in general, and exposed as an infiltrator, who cynically posed with Stein, then stabbed her in the back. It is time for Latino Lives Matter, and the radicals of Black Lives Matter, and all activist groups to work together to rid the community of infiltrators and people who would support Hillary, who called black children super-predators, and with her husband, made mandatory sentences, filling the prisons with blacks and brown people. No amount of money or circumstance would ever have me go door to door for her, and the dishonest and deceiving practices of Donna must be exposed!

Since that was written I exposed Donna who came to my neighborhood of Ybor for an anti Trump rally on video with members of HCC Greens, then the plot against me culminated.

Chapter III Standing Rock

I start this with my blog on my trip. https://alrsuarez.wordpress.com/2016/12/21/6-days-in-standing-rock-mecca-of-activists-revolution-of-diehards/

Image I took of the view from Sacred Stone camp, the original camp at Standing Rock Reservation.

In the most humbling experience of my life, I journeyed for the first time to Minneapolis en route to Standing Rock, to a site that has become a Mecca for activists. Minneapolis, has become a progressive hub or way for activists to fly in for cheap and then take a bus to Bismarck, a small town in North Dakota an hour from Standing Rock, but unlike Fargo ND, which is larger,   is the state capital. Minneapolis a Medina of sorts, a city where two of my heroes are from (Cheri Honkala & Jesse Ventura). It also happens to be the city where Sophia Wilanki,   who nearly lost her arm for the cause, was held in the hospital. Vanessa Dundon, who lost her vision in her right eye for the cause was also brought to the hospital there, where she hid out for a week, my experience and brief interview with her I will show later. Sophia actually left Minneapolis, the same day I arrived, on the 10th of December, which also happens to be the 5th year anniversary of my arrest at Occupy Boston, I ran into one of the 46 arrested with me while I was in Standing Rock, but I'll get into that later as well. I want to thank Jason & Jennifer, Trina & Jason, two couples in the city who helped me while I first got there and were quite hospitable in midwest fashion. Also Jason K, who gave a 20 dollar donation towards the trip, you can say the trip was made easier with the help of the three Jasons. One of the couples lived in Saint Paul, which is on the other side of the bridge from Minneapolis, its like St Pete to Tampa, or Mandan to Bismarck. While in Minneapolis I tried real Mexican food, as they have a Mexican community there, having mole for the first time. I could go on and on about the area but my focus is Standing Rock.

People came from tribes and nations throughout the world to Standing Rock. I met people from Norway, England, Bolivia, Mexico, Australia, Colombia and Canada. Out of the about 500 federally recognized tribes in the US, nearly 400 have participated in the Standing Rock rebellion. If you consider the non-federally recognized tribes, which were thought to have been wiped out, about 600 tribes took part. Of course tribes from other countries also came to show solidarity. A memer of the Sami for example in Norway I had encountered, as well of the Chacon from Bolivia. I always thought Bolivia, a nation that borders my father's country, consisted of only Aymara and Inca, but learned there are several other ethnicities there. The corporate media, since what I call the temporary victory, has actually started talking about the rebellion and what it is about, as not just via social media, but other means, Americans, and people throughout the world are learning about Standing Rock.

I arrived on Tuesday the 13th of December, a couple weekends before that, was the height when it came to the amount of people congregated at Standing Rock, this was when 2000 veterans came to defend Standing Rock including a Congresswoman, after the brutality of November 20th. With the entry of the veterans, many of them from the Veterans For Peace group, andd many reuniting with veterans who were already there, some of them, the diehards I met who stayed behind, even after the "victory", the numbers of those on the camps, were about 20,000, including 12,000 at main camp, and most of the others at Sacred Stone. By the time I got there, about 800 campers remained. Not just because the government said it would not grant the pipeline entry into Standing Rock, but the extreme weather and many of the chiefs, had convinced people to leave. Some perceived the chiefs insistance people leave as a selling out, while others clung to the words of Chief Chase Iron Eyes, who wanted people to stay. I was not able to meet this chief as he was traveling when I was there. But I met Chief Thomas, of the Apache, who told me his grandfather was from Florida, and that he was the great grandson of the Apache warrior Geronimo. People say the corporation can still build the pipeline through Standing Rock, just paying fines and still making a profit. Also Trump was an invester in the pipeline, and could make this victory go away.

I came from sub tropical weather in Florida to sub artic weather in North Dakota. At the greyhound station in Bismarck, called Jefferson station, a sister company, I found a veteran from Tenessee, of Spanish and Navajo origin, he did not know how he was going to get to Standing Rock from there, he was meaning to come before with the other veterans. Luckily I had a ride set up and we took a taxi to a diner and waited for it. When we were picked up, one of the people in the car was a Spaniard of Basque origin, a activist and reporter like me, who happened to be living in my hometown of Boston. He looked like a young Jeremy Irons, and he took it as a compliment, as we reminsced on the movie The Mission, where he and Deniro played together, it touches on the plight of the Guarani natives in Paraguay. Its funny as I was in Standing Rock I saw someone who looked like Richard Gere, and I was cold, I remembered The Pianist scene where Adrian Brody struggled to stay warm, and what do you know, when I walked into the school at Sacred Stone, there was a guy who looked just like him, beard and all, he said he got that a lot. Anyway, the Spaniard Inaki (the n is spelled with accent) told me how when he got to main camp for the first time and saw the teepees he cried, I did not, but tears came later.

Main camp is called Oceti Sakowen, Oceti can be pronouned Ocheti or Ochete, accentuating the e on the end. In means in one of the Sioux dialects,The 7 Tribes, during orientation we had 7 principles to follow. Interesting as 7 is my mother's favorite number. They say they are going to   change the name of Oceti camp to All Nations camp, it was originally a overflow camp as they ran out of room at Rosebud and Sacred Stone camps. A recurring theme was the Black Snake Sioux legend, that a Black Snake would come 7 generations (7 again) after the death of the Sioux warrior Crazy Horse, one of the natives who spoke on camp said a generation is averaged to 19 years, if you multiple that by 7 since 1877 when Crazy Horse was killed, that is 2017. 2017 could be the year it is determined if the Black Snake will be detroyed, or their nation will cease to exist. They said you can only kill the snake by starving it, and we must divest from the banks still supporting the pipeline. This man who spoke of the legend spoke from the Dome, which I called The Dome of the Rock (like the site in Jerusalem, and Rock like Standing Rock), it is in the center of camp, where orientation, and general meetings are held. Everyone can speak at the meetings, but it is done in a circular motion, just as the natives dance in a circular motion. I felt too humble to do anything but listen in these meetings. The man went on into how the Sioux language, has no swear words, and that the language comes from the animals, just as the natives learned to survive the winter from the animals. Wearing feathers and bear fur was the custom. The animals did not fear them then. It made me think of the story of Ernest Hemingway, and how he was a something of a Dr. Dolittle, liking to speak to animals. And yet he spoke to them at times in a Native American tongue, Hemingway then explained his great grandmother was Northern

Cheyenne, indeed I spoke to many people who were part native but very in touch with their roots.

People who met me in Standing Rock would say, he is a timid, quiet man. I of course am not, but I was humbled, in a trans, to a spiritual dimension that many peoples hearts drove them to come from afar to this sacred place in these crucial   times. The night we danced at the Dome, to native chants and drums,   I thought of the story of the Pawnee who entered camp. Like the Navajo who always fought the Hopi and Pueblo, but who are united for Standing Rock, the Pawnee and Sioux have been at it for centuries. I encountered Lakota, Dakota, several people of the Sioux nation. The Pawnee however, had been their sworn enemy. The Pawnee camp to the gate, and talked to a Sioux member, they said they would only enter if they had the peace pipe. The man at the gate called on the radio the elders, and they said he was on his own. They then proceded to have the peace pipe, and their unity was sealed. That is the importance of symbolism! I then thought about one of the police raids when a peace pipe was stolen, and tears came as we danced. To realize the sacrifice, and what an honor it was to be with these people. We danced holding hands, in a similar fashion as the Jews. I then thought of the DNA test I did before I got there, and how it showed am just as indigenous as I am Jewish.

Yes in the Dome inspite of firewood, we were cold, but we were then warmed by the love we had for one another. A hug and a prayer over lit sage were more common then a conversation or handshake. Am not religious, but in the food tent I ended up leading a prayer, I was not sure how to end it, and then was told to say All Nations, and I did, and then others shouted it its translation in indigenous tongue, and we enjoyed the native food prepared for us. And no, not everyone was vegan or vegetarian, typical of the hippie culture, many were meateaters, I had Elk and Buffalo while I was there, did not have any moments of hunger. The Elk was a jerky, and I informed people of how jerky was an invention of the Incas, as they called it Charqui, and used the freeze dry metod with llama meat. I also showed people my alpaca sweater, which was quite insolated, and felt pride in the part of my heritage which was Inca.

People should not make assumptions in these trips, and not be ethnocentric or judging when it comes to the cultue there. I was told going to Sacred Stone there would be snobby hippies, but when I went there they were incredibly receptive and positive. I enjoyed practising Spanish with those I could as well, and it was acceptable to speak in other languages besides English. I was lent a copy in Spanish of speeches by Subcomandante Marcos, and also lent a copy of The Open Veins of Latin America, by a writer I admire, but have never read Galeano's best book! I shared my cigar from Florida, with people including an elder, which is the custom, if a elder is present offer it to them, and they take it, whether they smoke it or not, sometimes not given back, luckily my cigar was and was able to enjoy the rest of it. Coffee and chocolate are not indigenous to the land, but tobacco is, and is a sacred substance to the natives. Also chivalry is real in the native struggle, women, children and elders eat first. In the Dome I ran into Rita, arrested with me at Occupy Boston, and I smiled and hugged her when I saw her, and our energies connected. We spoke briefly, I mentioned of all days I arrived in Minneapolis on my way to N Dakota on December 10th.

I will now go into how I met the incredibly brave Navajo woman Vanessa Dundon. I was told the tent Inaki brought me to, to sleep, had several tent mates, including Vanessa, also known as Sioux Z. I took a nap after a long trip in the tent, suddenly I awoke to the sound of a radio, I thought, the cops? And a woman emerged in front of me with her eye covered, it was Vanessa! I told her what an honor it was to meet her, because of Sophia's and her's sacrifice, it convinced me to finally come up there to join the cause. She told me she liked my boots, and thats when I discovered she could see out her other eye, as I was under the impression she was completly blind. She asked if I wanted to go to the casino with her, and I said yes, I met her brother, and we stopped in the veterans camp on the way. The casino is not where activists go to gamble but use internet, or get a cheap hotel room for a break from the camp's cold. At the veterans camp a photographer said she liked the pirate look of Vanessa, luckily she took it as a compliment, but then Vanessa told her who she was, and you should have seen the change of expression on the lady's face! I was going to interview Vanessa at the casino but she was not feeling well, we did it later. My second night on camp, by the morning I had frost bite on my face, and   a comrade took pity on me and put coconot oil on my face. I then decided to go back to the community center for a warm bed as I had been there previously for a hot shower, I eventually brought my stuff there and the remainder of my days slept there, but never had trouble getting rides and always went to camp or some activitiy the days I was there.

Vanessa later wrote me on fb her room number. I figured that meant she was feeling better and could ask her some questions. To my dismay she opened the door, and went back to bed in pain. A medic came to check in on her, and I discovered almost a month after injury, she was not on medication! She lost her ID, and could not get a prescription. So while they were working it out, they said she could get tylenol. So I went to see the doctor I knew at community center, and got the meds she needed with instructions, and returned to the casino. She then took it, and eventually I got her bagpack she left on camp with her computer back as well.She felt better, and we proceded with the interview. It is amazing what one person can do being at the right place at the right time, I had no idea I was going to meet her, let alone help her, that out of 800 campers, my tent would be the tent where her things were! And unlike Sophia, who deserved all the respect in the world, Vanessa, a proud Native American woman is still staying out there after the brutal attack of November 20th!

What brought you out there?

Vanessa: "When I saw the picture of the girl mauled by the dog, I had to come out, the picture ended up being fake, but it still brought me out."

Has the mass media been covering what happened to you?

Vanessa: "Only the LA Times reached out to me. I went to Minneapolis for a week after the attack to hide out. The media and government are bought out. That is why in general they do not cover well whats going on here."

What do you think of the so-called victory?

Vanessa: "Its not over yet. Its a ploy tactic to send the Vets back. Until we walk across the bridge peacefully, and the drill pads stop, then it will be a victory. Dont forget about us. We are still here, in the harsh cold, we are warriors over here."

Just that encounter alone made the whole trip worth while. But I did other interviews. One of them too brief to post, but I want to give kudos to Vinni Lomeli, who helped set up my tent after being introduced to by Inaki. It was a joy speaking Spanish to him, and watching him dance in the Dome. Also want to mention Miguel Elliott, I lost the notes of our interview in the rush to catch a ride, he constructs homes and has some awesome ideas about permanent structures, and how they can be used on reservations, for a self-sufficient society, which already has shown some success at Sacred Stone and other areas he has worked. My interview I was able to salvage, was at Sacred Stone, Inaki introduced me to a very interesting person. She is Australian with Colombian origins, and also with some Mapuche origin, from southern South America, she remarked how she moved from the jungles of Australia to the cold of N Dakota, what a distance and change! We talked about the travel of Polynesian people to the Amazon, how they shared   a heritage. How Mapuchee had similarities with the Aborigin. How people end up there, or end up staying, is quite interesting. So after meeting this woman, named Patricia Villegas, at the casino, she told me to look for her at the love kitchen, at Sacred Stone where it all started! We conducted out interview from the soon to be finished structure called the "Sacred Stone Community School", as unlike on other parts of camp, I saw after passing through Rosebud, children there. Among the people I encountered was Jeane Dorado, a woman of Mexican origin who will be principal of the school, and has a gorgeous 2 year old daughter accompanying her. She was the one who lent me the Eduardo Galeano book, but did not get a chance to interview her.

How long have you been out here?

Patricia: "3 weeks."

What did you come out for?

Patricia: "Came to help with a prayer in my heart, to contribute to change consciousness."

What will happen to those that leave after experiencing things out here?

Patricia: "There has been long-term impact for those returning."

And so recurring themes went on for the remainder of my stay at Standing Rock, like how the natives see things as relationships, not transactions. As we are all on motherearth, or what the Incas called Pachamama. I also talked with a Native American on the fact that European disease, like common cold, cough, flu, cancer, were unknown to the Natives. Thy either died in battle or of old age well into their 80s or 90s. I thought of how these civilizations flourished, who were the real savages? Things will never be the same for me, those who have gone to Standing Rock and felt what I felt know, that it never leaves you. I hope to apply these principles here in Florida as we fight the Sabal pipeline, as this fight continues in other areas inspired the great spirit, Standing Rock, my transformation has just begun...

*Since this was written, Vanessa did talk to LA Times, a doctor read the article, and she got a second opinion, she went to Chicago and got surgery on her eye, and it looks like part of her vision in that eye will be recovered! She has since left N Dakota to go home, although am sure she will return. Sophia used part of the money she raised to help other victims from November 20th. Vanessa also offered her hotel room to a comrade of mine, I guess when she left there was still days paid on it. Unfortunately, the unity I sought upon returning home with my fellow activists I have not been able to get, nor a ride to the anti-Sabal camps down here. There are other details of my trip there I have mentioned in fb posts, and I plan for my book, as you cannot write about the environment without talking about the Native Americans. One of the names of the tribes I misspelled, which I have since corrected, am sorry if anyone was offended by this.

Chapter V Unity

The importance of unity, especially in emerging groups or political parties, is of utmost importance. This chapter is brief but concise, concision is vital on this point. Strength, and confidence, can be found from unity for a common cause. Division weakens and makes us lose our self-confidence. A united front or coalition is an external unity, this chapter will discuss the internal. One must not strive to be controversial, but one must not avoid controversy when the issue matters to them. The ancient Athenians were wise to make it illegal to avoid controversy. In their democratic politics, every year they would disgrace the most unpopular politician in the city-state or Republic of Athens to exile, as a result the representatives of the people were always desperate for their support.

A people can only make a demand of those that supposedly represent us with one voice however, with unity, as we are not in such an idealistic society as the Athenians. This society of course had its contradictions, it had slavery. It took a Greek, Spartacus, a slave, to bring the Roman Empire to its knees. Our new society must be inherently anti imperialist, therefore must have Libertarian and Socialist leanings, protecting liberties, and being egalitarian, and of course must be Green at heart, no system without protection of eco-system.

In essence, the society we struggle to build, must come about just that, building, not destroying, destroying others or building walls, but building bridges...

Chapter IV

History

It is quasi obsessive, certainly a passionate emphasis on my part, to bring historical parallels to basically anything I discuss or write in the political realm. We must learn from history to apply to the current and future, the good and the bad, the mistakes and the successes, the short and long-term effects, all must be considered. Certainly, if you look at recent history, in-spite of some current problems in Argentina and Venezuela, with South America, it gives you hope that they are reaching the great Liberator's dream Bolivar of unity soon, an integration of Latin American states that is against all empires, whether from the North or Europe. Diversity in the city where I write from Miami, makes it a melting pot of Latin America, and yet this stereotype that us Latins are all nationalists and hate one another or the countries or governments that represent us, is a false narrative. The youth are rebelling against the old order. Case in point Cuba.

Figures as high as 95% of Cuban American millennials are against the economic embargo against their nation. This in part convinced Obama to commence normalization with Raul Castro's government. The restrictions on travel to see family, and use of American dollars from American visitors (still not called tourists since US Congress technically has not lifted the blockade) as the restrictions applied to us as well, have been relaxed. And it happened on the date of December 17th, when Bolivar died, I think this deal put a smile on his face, was more beneficial for the Cubans. It also happens to be my mother's birthday, who later this year wants to go to Cuba with me, I plan to go before that as well, and see what is left of Socialism, which on the down side, is at risk with this deal. Pythagorean numerologists may find significance for that date. There are certain freedoms lacking in Cuba that they have in places like Venezuela, free speech, but they have maintained against all odds a Socialist based economy, rights we do not have here, public health care, and public university up to PHD.

Jose Marti later after Bolivar, Bolivar being his hero, tried to free Cuba as Fidel did, he lived for a time where I did in Tampa, and Cubans there tending to be more progressive than Miami on all levels. Only Marti's attempt was against the Spanish Empire, he did however see the dangers of US influence in the region. This culminated in the late 1950s with Batista's regime, hence the rise of Castro. It is also a recent history that must be looked at. Did Fidel have a cult of personality? I do not think he had an obvious one like Stalin did back in the Soviet Union upon consolidating power. Unlike Che Guevara after his death, there were no currency with his face on it, no town or city named after him. However, on a more subtle level, he did indeed have that cult, and used the image of Che, a true revolutionary and man of principle and self-sacrifice, to increase is own image in an opportunistic way. Recently, when I interviewed Ray Suarez, we talked about how Pedro Albizu Campos was similar to Marti, both men being of letters and wanting to free their Caribbean nations. Che often talked of both men, as Pedro was alive at the same time as Che, and in 65' was released from prison in Puerto Rican paralyzed from the constant torture he received over the years, dying soon after.

When you look at the history of revolutions, you have to realize, the US is a young nation, but the revolution here sparked others. First the French, then the Russian, but anti-Monarchist movements much like in North America, against the British Crown. Each revolution purportedly brought about republics. Even the Soviet Union essentially called itself a republic. The republican idea, like the democratic, stems from the Greeks. I often refer to them, it is hard not to when discussing political history. The economic war today against Greece, being conducted primarily by other European nations to the North, I find a new form of colonialism, turning Greece into Africa, and turning their progressive leaders on their people. The situation in Spain however gives me some hope, and again I think of the Spanish Civil War and the eternal lessons we can learn from that, as we have a similar leader in Trump to Franco, a man surrounded by fascists, who is putting the working class disarray in this country like it was back in the 1930s.

Chapter IIV Conclusion

My faith in the Green cause, in-spite of setbacks and seeming for all odds to be against my people and me, is stronger than ever. In Florida alone, the battle-ground state, 4 times more people voted for our candidate for president, Dr. Jill Stein, than in 2012. Nationwide it was 2 times. The old narrative or myth that you must vote Dem in a swing state for the "lesser evil" is fading away.

A new generation of Greens, especially from the college campuses and protest/prayer camps against pipelines, including the one here Sabal, will form more than a coalition for an alliance, of Native Americans, blacks, Latinos, working class white, the downtrodden in general, to end the tyranny of the ruling class, the elite, or what is commonly referred to as the 1%. Am a realist, but am also filled with optimism, as I saw incredible unity in Standing Rock, in-spite of generations of fighting between tribes, they came together for water, for life. Perhaps this should have been mentioned more in the Unity chapter, but it was more about internal unity among Greens in forming an opposition. I want to state that everyone has an agenda, the question is whether the agenda is hidden, or is being imposed, we must be open and transparent, but also strategic, the strategy based on principles. Our opposition must essentially get more, give it to the people, and be a true democracy, learning from the past, building the new world in the present, for a better future for all our children, as I said that night in 2011 when we were arrested at Occupy, as mentioned in my first book. Let this my 8th book, as my late sister was born on January 8th, be a success, for my niece to grow up and read all my writings, and it make her be a better human and citizen of this world...

www.ingramcontent.com/pod-product-compliance
Lightning Source LLC
Chambersburg PA
CBHW050931290526
45792CB00002B/974